The Sayings
of Jesus

The English translation of the Sayings Gospel Q presented here is that of James M. Robinson, based on the work of the International Q Project, published in *The Critical Edition of Q: Synopsis, including the Gospels of Matthew and Luke, Mark and Thomas, with English, German, and French Translations of Q and Thomas* (Minneapolis: Fortress Press; and Leuven: Peeters, 2000) and in shortened form in *The Sayings Gospel Q in Greek and English with Parallels from the Gospels of Mark and Thomas* (Leuven: Peeters, 2001; and Minneapolis: Fortress Press, 2002).

The Sayings of Jesus

The Sayings Gospel Q
in English

Edited by
James M. Robinson

Fortress Press
Minneapolis

THE SAYINGS OF JESUS
The Sayings Gospel Q in English

Cover and book design: Joseph Bonyata
Cover graphic: Andreas Rentsch.
Copyright © nonstøck inc. Used by permission.

ISBN 0-8006-3451-9

The paper used in this publication meets the minimum
requirements of American National Standard for Information Sciences—Permanence of Paper for Printed
Library Materials, ANSI Z329.48-1984.

Manufactured in the U.S.A.   AF 1-3451

06 05   04   03 02 1 2 3 4 5 6 7 8 9 10

Contents

Foreword

What Is the Sayings Gospel Q?

A Sayings Gospel, in distinction from a Narrative Gospel, contains mainly sayings ascribed to Jesus, with hardly any of the stories so familiar to us from the four Narrative Gospels of the New Testament.

The Sayings Gospel Q is even older than the Gospels in the New Testament. In fact, it is the oldest Gospel known! Yet it is not in the New Testament itself—rather, it was known to, and used by, the authors of the Gospels of Matthew and Luke in the eighties and nineties of the first century when they composed their Gospels. But then it was lost from sight and only rediscovered in 1838, embedded in Matthew and Luke.

After all, Q is a product of the Jewish Jesus movement that continued to proclaim his message in Galilee and Syria for years to come, but from which practically no first-century texts have survived. The New Testament is mainly a Gentile collection, and hence only preserves the sources of Gentile churches.

This is clearest in the case of Matthew, the canonical Gospel that grew out of the Q movement, marking the point when it finally merged into the Gentile churches. Matthew 3-11 is primarily oriented to vindicating the Jewish Gospel Q, whereupon Matthew 12-28 simply edits and copies out the oldest Gentile Gospel, Mark. The Great Commission with which Matthew concludes (Matthew 28:18-20) makes this Gospel an ecumenical text: It not only authorizes the Gentile church's mission ("make disciples of all nations"), but also the Jewish church's focus on the sayings of Jesus found in Q ("teaching them to observe all that I have commanded you").

Conversely, the Gentile Gospel that most fully represents the final triumph of Gentile churches, Luke, has simply imbedded Q into the Markan Gentile Gospel. And Luke continued with a second volume, the Acts of the Apostles, where the history of the Gentile churches very soon tends to become the history of the churches as a whole.

One can identify Q sayings in Matthew and Luke by a rule of thumb: Sayings (and a few stories) that occur in Matthew and Luke but not in Mark, or in Matthew and Luke in a very different form from that in Mark (for example, the temptation story in Matt 4:1-11, parallel Luke 4:1-13; see Mark 1:12-13), probably come from Q.

The Greek Composition of Q

Although Jesus' mother tongue was Aramaic, his sayings had been largely translated into Greek for missionary purposes. Then they were collected into small clusters, which were eventually brought together into the Sayings Gospel Q. The sometimes very high degree of verbal identity in the Q sayings of Matthew and Luke makes it apparent that they were working from a shared Greek text. For each could not have translated from Aramaic into such highly similar, often identical, Greek, if they had translated independently of one other (for example, Matt 3:7-10, parallel Luke 3:7-9).

At another place (citing Q by reference to Luke's chapter and verse numbers: Q 12:27), the fact of a written Greek text of Q is strikingly attested by the presence of a Greek scribal error. Both Matthew and Luke (Matt 6:25-33, parallel Luke 12:22b-31), and therefore Q, list in quite parallel form three tasks that ravens and lilies, free of anxiety, do not perform, as role models for humans to imitate, indicating that they too are free of anxiety: Ravens do not sow, or reap, or gather into barns. But in the case of the lilies, Q reads: "how they grow: They do not work nor do they spin." Here the first of the three tasks anxiety-free lilies do not perform is neither a negative statement, nor a verb naming a task involved in making cloth. But a very slight change in the Greek lettering produces the meaning: "They do not card, nor do they work, nor do they spin." The formulation "not card" is not just a convincing conjecture, but is faintly attested, as an erased original reading, in an ancient manuscript of Matthew (6:28b), preserved down through the centuries in the Monastery of St. Catherine at Mount Sinai (now in the British Library in London), and in a Greek fragment of saying 36 of the *Gospel of Thomas*, in Papyrus Oxyrhynchus 655, preserved in the dry sands of Egypt near the town of Nag Hammadi (now in the Houghton Library of Harvard University).

The Disappearance of Q

The loss of much of what may have been written in the earliest churches should not surprise us, since no New Testament manuscripts of the first century survive (and only a very few small fragments from the second). In 1 Corinthians 5:9 and 2 Corinthians 2:3-4, 9, Paul refers to other letters he wrote to Corinth, which are either completely lost or incorporated into the two canonical Corinthian letters. (This is analogous to Q surviving only as incorporated into Matthew and Luke.)

The disappearance of Q may have been facilitated by scribes not making new copies during the second century. For the canonizing process that was going on at the time involved choosing what should, and what should not, be used for community purposes. In Matthew and Luke, the Q sayings had been rephrased to avoid misunderstandings, and updated so as to fit their new situations and understanding of what Jesus had really meant. For this very practical reason, churches would have commissioned scribes to make copies of Matthew and Luke, rather than copying Q, which had fallen into disuse.

Such creeds as the Apostles' Creed, which developed out of the second-century baptismal liturgy of Rome, bypassed completely the sayings of Jesus ("born of the virgin Mary, suffered under Pontius Pilate"). This provided no basis for canonizing Sayings Gospels, such as Q and the *Gospel of Thomas* (the latter was lost for more than 1,500 years and only discovered in 1945). But the creeds did validate as canonical the narrative Gospels Matthew, Mark, Luke, and John, because of their emphasis on the cross and resurrection.

Memorable Sayings of Jesus in Q

The Sayings Gospel Q contains some of the most memorable of Jesus' sayings. To mention only a few: The most familiar Q text is the Lord's Prayer (Q 11:2b-4). Q presents it in a more original form than what we use in our liturgy today. For what we know by heart is Matthew's enlargement of the Q Prayer: Matthew 6:9-13.

Q also preserves for us most of the Sermon on the Mount: The beatitudes (Q 6:20-23); the love of enemies (Q 6:27-28, 35c-d); turning the other cheek, giving the shirt off one's back, going the second mile, giving, expecting nothing in return (Q 6:29-30); the Golden Rule (Q 6:31); the tree known by its fruit (Q 6:43-45). This is all in Q's early draft of the Sermon (Q 6:20-49), to which Matthew has added even more of the oldest Q clusters of sayings to produce his considerably enlarged Sermon on the Mount with which we are familiar (Matthew 5-7): Not only the Lord's Prayer, but also the certainty of the answer to prayer (ask, seek, knock, for a caring Father does provide, Q 11:9-13); storing up treasures in heaven (Q 12:33-34); being free from anxiety like ravens and lilies (Q 12:22b-31); the sound eye rather than the evil eye (Q 11:33-35).

Q has many other important and familiar sayings, such as taking up one's cross (Q 14:27), and losing one's life to save it (Q 17:33). Q also preserves a number of well-known parables, such as the mustard seed (Q 13:18-19); the yeast (Q 13:20-21); the invited dinner guests (Q 14:16-23); the lost sheep (Q 15:4-7); the lost coin (Q 15:8-10); and the talents (Q used the much smaller coin, "minas": Q 19:12-26). All such sayings and parables are familiar to us, since they are found in Matthew and Luke. But we know them only because Matthew and Luke found them in Q, and thus handed them down to us in the New Testament.

The Image of Jesus in Q

The image of Jesus one gets from the Sayings Gospel Q is primarily that of the authoritative speaker of his sayings. Doing what he says is really all that counts: "Why do you call me: Master, Master, and do not do what I say?" (Q 6:46). For it is only the person who hears his sayings and acts on them who will stand in the judgment (Q 6:47-49).

Jesus refers to himself in Q largely by means of a Semitic idiom for "human," literally "son of man," or, more accurately, "son of humanity" (Q 6:22; 7:34; 9:58; 11:30; 12:8, 10). Toward the end of Q, the sayings tend to focus increasingly on Jesus returning from heaven, and then the idiom is used more as a title to refer to him as a heavenly figure (Q 12:40; 17:24, 26, 30): "Son of Humanity." But Jesus' own focus was on God reigning ("the kingdom of God"), not on himself.

John had predicted "One to Come," as the final arrival of God for judgment (Q 3:16b-17). The first part of Q (Q 3-7) is carefully structured to prove that it is Jesus who fulfills this prophecy, even though on the surface he hardly fits John's description. For in Q 7:18-23 John sends a delegation to ask if Jesus is indeed that "One to Come." Jesus answers in the affirmative and lists as evidence his healings (Q 7:22), for which reason the healing of the centurion's boy immediately precedes (Q 7:1-10). This list is climaxed by reference to Jesus giving good news to the poor, which is a reference back to Q's early draft of the Sermon on the Mount (Q 6:20-49). For it had begun: "Blessed are the poor."

Other titles are also used of Jesus, such as "Son of God" (Q 3:22; 4:3, 9; 10:22). This title was initially used of any "son of God," a God-like person who loves even one's enemies (Q 6:27-28). For Jesus' remarkable view of God was that he gives sunshine and rain equally to bad and good persons (Q 6:35). Those who act similarly show that God is their Father and they his children.

"Lord" is the standard epithet for God in the Greek translation of the Hebrew Bible, and so is of course used of God in Q (Q 4:12, 8; 10:2, 21; 13:35; 16:13). But the same word is also used in its secular meaning of a human "master" (Q 12:42, 43, 46; 13:25; 14:21; 19:16, 18, 20) or "teacher" (Q 6:46; 9:59). Of course such human designations acquired progressively a higher implication, when referring to or even just implying Jesus.

Perhaps the most striking thing about epithets for Jesus in Q is the complete absence of the title "Christ." This fits the absence of a birth narrative in Bethlehem, the prophesied birthplace of the Messiah.

The Death of Jesus in Q

The oldest theology addressed to Gentile believers to have survived is the collection of letters of Paul, which date from the fifties. But for Paul, the center of the gospel message was Jesus' cross and resurrection, not his sayings, which Paul himself had not heard. Since Paul's mission was to "Gentile sinners" (Gal 2:15), he focused on Jesus' death as compensation for human sin. So, for us as modern Gentile Christians, Paul's message has tended to obscure Jesus' own message, though Jesus' sayings had, after all, been preferred by his own disciples.

Of course the Q people knew of Jesus' death. But they saw it more as the inevitable culmination of the activity of God's Wisdom, who had sent messengers to Israel down through the course of biblical history, prophets who had often been required to give their lives for God's cause (Q 11:47-51; 12:4-5; 13:34-35). In spite of Jesus' terrible death, his message of complete trust in God was resumed by his disciples in the Q movement, as being as true as ever—their way of bringing to expression what we express as Easter faith.

Jesus' Jewish Disciples in Q

The Sayings Gospel Q, though on the surface only reporting about Jesus, also reveals almost all we know about Jesus' Jewish followers of the first generation in Galilee. For since the New Testament, as we have it, is a collection almost exclusively of Gentile texts, it contains only occasional passing references to Jewish churches.

There is something of a biographical cast in the early part of Q (baptism, temptation, inaugural sermon, healing of the centurion's boy, delegation from John). On the other hand, the sayings of Jesus also mirror something like the sequence of the Q community's own experience. This begins with what may well be the oldest cluster of Jesus' sayings in the inaugural sermon, then the Jewish mission, its very limited success, the resultant alienation from the Jewish community, and finally the expectation of final vindication at the last judgment.

Paul gained acceptance for his Gentile mission from the "pillars" of the church in Jerusalem (James, Cephas, and John: Gal 2:1-10), though this amicable division of labor soon broke down (Gal 2:11-21), when Peter and the disciples from Jerusalem tried to "judaize" Gentile disciples (Gal 2:14) by subjecting them to Jewish cultic law, such as circumcision and segregated table fellowship. Paul withstood the claims of any other "gospel" than his own (Gal 1:6-12), which served to cast a shadow over the divergent message and practice of those from Jerusalem.

Actually, the disciples of the Q movement do not seem to have been these leaders stationed in Jerusalem. For the "apostles" and the "twelve" are not mentioned in Q, either by title or by name, nor does Q make any reference to the problems that were central issues in the debate with Paul. The Q people would seem to have been the disciples of Jesus who had stayed behind in Galilee. Some were originally itinerant (like the "workers" mentioned in Q 10:2 and 7), wandering from door to door with Jesus' message, as is evident from the Mission Instructions in Q 10:2-16.

Yet the lack of success in winning over appreciable numbers of Jewish converts led to disillusionment, over against an invidious awareness of the success of the Gentile mission (Q 13:29-30; 14:11-23). The tone became judgmental toward Israel (Q 3:7-9; 10:10-15; 11:23, 42-51; 13:24-28, 34-35; 22:28, 30). Indeed, the destruction of Jerusalem and its temple was interpreted (Q 13:34-35) as divine punishment on "this generation" (Q 7:31; 11:29 twice, 30, 31, 32, 50, 51), and especially on its leaders, upon whom "woes" were pronounced (Q 11:42-48). The breaking of family ties (Q 12:49-53; 14:26), the rigors of the primitive lifestyle (Q 12:4-7; 14:27; 17:33), even persecution (Q 6:22-23; 12:8-12), surely made quitting the Jesus movement a live option (Q 14:34-35). The dominant lifestyle was probably becoming less itinerant and more sedentary (like the "son of peace" mentioned in Q 10:6) as time went on.

The "final" Greek text of Q, that is to say, the text shared by Matthew and Luke, probably dates from around the time of the war with Rome (since Q 13:34-35 seems to envisage the destruction of Jerusalem in 70 C.E.). Under such desperate circumstances, the Matthean merger into the more successful Gentile church was a rather inevitable outcome.

Thus it may be understandable that by Luke's time these remaining Galilean disciples could be largely overlooked in the Acts of the Apostles. For the description of the mission there, "from Jerusalem and in all Judea and Samaria and to the end of the earth" (Acts 1:8), simply bypassed Galilee, with only one reference later in Acts (9:31) to a church in Galilee being built up. Nor can one find in Acts any attestation for disciples still proclaiming Jesus' sayings. The Sayings Gospel Q thus supplements Acts in a very central way concerning what we know about the first generation of the Jesus movement.

The Jewish-Christian Dialogue

In the contemporary Jewish-Christian dialogue, it is very important to recognize this unbreakable bond between Jews and Christians: Jesus was a Jew, as were his first disciples. What Jesus and they proclaimed was a message by and for the Jews. It was such an idealized message that it presents a real challenge for modern Jews and Christians alike. Yet it is a message that we all can join in seeking to live up to. Its basis is trust in the same God.

—James M. Robinson

The Sayings Gospel Q
in English Translation

The translation of Q that is supplied here is intended to be readable by the general public. For this reason the text is not cluttered with marks indicating the various kinds and degrees of certainty or uncertainty. Those wishing such detailed information may find it in *The Critical Edition of Q* (2000), or in the somewhat simplified and abbreviated form in *The Sayings Gospel Q in Greek and English* (2001, 2002). Therefore the translation presented here is encumbered only rarely, with markings of three kinds: If there is a high degree of uncertainty about a particular word or phrase, no text is provided, but the place is marked with three dots ... indicating that there was some text here. Two dots .. indicate that it is even uncertain whether anything at all was here. Parentheses ( ) are used where the text had to be emended, or where only the gist or train of thought, but not the actual language, could be provided. The chapter and verse numbers of Q follow the Gospel of Luke. For example, the reference to Q 6:22 indicates the Q version of the saying found in Luke 6:22 (and in its Matthean parallel, Matt 5:11). In one instance, a Q saying is only in Matthew; it is listed between the immediately preceding and following Q sayings that are in Luke: Q 6:29↔30/Matt 5:41 means that this Matthean verse belongs in Q between Q 6:29 and Q 6:30.

Opening Line
(... Jesus ...)

Q 3:0

The Introduction of John

2b (...) John[3a] (...) all the region of the Jordan (...).

Q 3:2b-3a

John's Announcement of Judgment

7 He said to the crowds coming to be baptized: Snakes' litter! Who warned you to run from the impending rage? [8] So bear fruit worthy of repentance, and do not presume to tell yourselves: We have as forefather Abraham! For I tell you: God can produce children for Abraham right out of these rocks! [9] And the ax already lies at the root of the trees. So every tree not bearing healthy fruit is to be chopped down and thrown on the fire.

Q 3:7-9

John and the One to Come

16b I baptize you in water, but the one to come after me is more powerful than I, whose sandals I am not fit to take off. He will baptize you in holy Spirit and fire. [17] His pitchfork is in his hand, and he will clear his threshing floor and gather the wheat into his granary, but the chaff he will burn on a fire that can never be put out.

Q 3:16b-17

The Baptism of Jesus

21 .. Jesus ... baptized, heaven opened .., *22* and .. the Spirit ... upon him ... Son ... .

Q 3:21-22

The Temptations of Jesus

1 And Jesus was led into the wilderness by the Spirit *2* to be tempted by the devil. And he ate nothing for forty days; .. he became hungry. *3* And the devil told him: If you are God's Son, order that these stones become loaves. *4* And Jesus answered him: It is written: A person is not to live only from bread.

9 The devil took him along to Jerusalem and put him on the tip of the temple and told him: If you are God's Son, throw yourself down. *10* For it is written: He will command his angels about you, *11* and on their hands they will bear you, so that you do not strike your foot against a stone. *12* And Jesus in reply told him: It is written: Do not put to the test the Lord your God.

5 And the devil took him along to a very high mountain and showed him all the kingdoms of the world and their splendor, *6* and told him: All these I will give you, *7* if you bow down before me. *8* And in reply Jesus told him: It is written: Bow down to the Lord your God, and serve only him.

13 And the devil left him.

Q 4:1-4, 9-12, 5-8, 13

Nazara

16 (...) Nazara (...).

Q 4:16

Beatitudes for the Poor, Hungry, and Mourning

20 (...) And raising his eyes to his disciples he said: Blessed are you poor, for God's reign is for you. ²¹ Blessed are you who hunger, for you will eat your fill. Blessed are you who mourn, for you will be consoled.

Q 6:20-21

The Beatitude for the Persecuted

22 Blessed are you when they insult and persecute you, and say every kind of evil against you because of the son of humanity. ²³ Be glad and exult, for vast is your reward in heaven. For this is how they persecuted the prophets who were before you.

Q 6:22-23

Love Your Enemies

27 Love your enemies ²⁸ and pray for those persecuting you, ^{35c-d} so that you may become sons of your Father, for he raises his sun on bad and good and rains on the just and unjust.

Q 6:27-28, 35c-d

Renouncing One's Own Rights

29 The one who slaps you on the cheek, offer him the other as well; and to the person wanting to take you to court and get your shirt, turn over to him the coat as well. *29 ↔ 30/Matt 5:41* And the one who conscripts you for one mile, go with him a second. *30* To the one who asks of you, give; and from the one who borrows, do not ask back what is yours.

Q 6:29, 29↔30/Matt 5:41, 30

The Golden Rule

31 And the way you want people to treat you, that is how you treat them.   *Q 6:31*

Impartial Love

32 .. If you love those loving you, what reward do you have? Do not even tax collectors do the same? *34* And if you lend to those from whom you hope to receive, what (reward do) you (have)? Do not even the Gentiles do the same?

Q 6:32, 34

Being Full of Pity like Your Father

36 Be full of pity, just as your Father .. is full of pity.   *Q 6:36*

Not Judging

37 .. Do not pass judgment, so you are not judged. For with what judgment you pass judgment, you will be judged. *38* And with the measurement you use to measure out, it will be measured out to you.

Q 6:37-38

The Blind Leading the Blind

39 Can a blind person show the way to a blind person? Will not both fall into a pit?

Q 6:39

The Disciple and the Teacher

40 A disciple is not superior to the teacher. It is enough for the disciple that he become like his teacher.

Q 6:40

The Speck and the Beam

41 And why do you see the speck in your brother's eye, but the beam in your own eye you overlook? *42* How can you say to your brother: Let me throw out the speck from your eye, and just look at the beam in your own eye? Hypocrite, first throw out from your own eye the beam, and then you will see clearly to throw out the speck in your brother's eye.

Q 6:41-42

The Tree Is Known by its Fruit

43 .. No healthy tree bears rotten fruit, nor on the other hand does a decayed tree bear healthy fruit. [44] For from the fruit the tree is known. Are figs picked from thorns, or grapes from thistles? [45] The good person from one's good treasure casts up good things, and the evil person from the evil treasure casts up evil things. For from exuberance of heart one's mouth speaks.

Q 6:43-45

Not Just Saying Master, Master

46 .. Why do you call me: Master, Master, and do not do what I say?

Q 6:46

Houses Built on Rock or Sand

47 Everyone hearing my sayings and acting on them [48] is like a person who built one's house on bedrock; and the rain poured down and the flash-floods came, and the winds blew and pounded that house, and it did not collapse, for it was founded on bedrock. [49] And everyone who hears my sayings and does not act on them is like a person who built one's house on the sand; and the rain poured down and the flash-floods came, and the winds blew and battered that house, and promptly it collapsed, and its fall was devastating.

Q 6:47-49

The Centurion's Faith in Jesus' Word

1 And it came to pass when he .. ended these sayings, he entered Capernaum. *3* There came to him a centurion exhorting him and saying: My boy (is) doing badly. And he said to him: Am I, by coming, to heal him? *6b-c* And in reply the centurion said: Master, I am not worthy for you to come under my roof; *7* but say a word, and let my boy be healed. *8* For I too am a person under authority, with soldiers under me, and I say to one: Go, and he goes, and to another: Come, and he comes, and to my slave: Do this, and he does it. *9* But Jesus, on hearing, was amazed, and said to those who followed: I tell you, not even in Israel have I found such faith. *10* (..)

Q 7:1, 3, 6b-9, 10

John's Inquiry about the One to Come

18 And John, on hearing about all these things, sending through his disciples, *19* said to him: Are you the one to come, or are we to expect someone else? *22* And in reply he said to them: Go report to John what you hear and see: The blind regain their sight and the lame walk around, the skin-diseased are cleansed and the deaf hear, and the dead are raised, and the poor are evangelized. *23* And blessed is whoever is not offended by me.

Q 7:18-19, 22-23

John — More than a Prophet

24 And when they had left, he began to talk to the crowds about John: What did you go out into the wilderness to look at? A reed shaken by the wind? *25* If not, what *did* you go out to see? A person arrayed in finery? Look, those wearing finery are in kings' houses. *26* But then what did you go out to see? A prophet? Yes, I tell you, even more than a prophet! *27* This is the one about whom it has been written: Look, I am sending my messenger ahead of you, who will prepare your path in front of you. *28* I tell you: There has not arisen among women's offspring anyone who surpasses John. Yet the least significant in God's kingdom is more than he.

Q 7:24-28

For and Against John

29 For John came to you .. the tax collectors and ... (responded positively) *30* but the (religious authorities rejected) him.

Q 7: 29-30

This Generation and the Children of Wisdom

31 .. To what am I to compare this generation and what is it like? *32* It is like children seated in the market-places, who, addressing the others, say: We fluted for you, but you would not dance; we wailed, but you would not cry. *33* For John came, neither eating nor drinking, and you say: He has a demon!

[34] The son of humanity came, eating and drinking, and you say: Look! A person who is a glutton and drunkard, a chum of tax collectors and sinners! [35] But Wisdom was vindicated by her children.

Q 7:31-35

Confronting Potential Followers

57 And someone said to him: I will follow you wherever you go. [58] And Jesus said to him: Foxes have holes, and birds of the sky have nests; but the son of humanity does not have anywhere he can lay his head. [59] But another said to him: Master, permit me first to go and bury my father. [60] But he said to him: Follow me, and leave the dead to bury their own dead.

Q 9:57-60

Workers for the Harvest

2 He said to his disciples: The harvest is plentiful, but the workers are few. So ask the Lord of the harvest to dispatch workers into his harvest.

Q 10:2

Sheep among Wolves

3 Be on your way! Look, I send you like sheep in the midst of wolves.

Q 10:3

No Provisions

4 Carry no purse, nor knapsack, nor shoes, nor stick, and greet no one on the road.

Q 10:4

What to Do in Houses and Towns

5 Into whatever house you enter, first say: Peace to this house! *6* And if a son of peace be there, let your peace come upon him; but if not, let your peace return upon you. *7* And at that house remain, eating and drinking whatever they provide, for the worker is worthy of one's reward. Do not move around from house to house. *8* And whatever town you enter and they take you in, eat what is set before you. *9* And cure the sick there, and say to them: God's reign has reached unto you.

Q 10:5-9

Response to a Town's Rejection

10 But into whatever town you enter and they do not take you in, on going out from that town, *11* shake off the dust from your feet. *12* I tell you: For Sodom it shall be more bearable on that day than for that town.

Q 10:10-12

Woes against Galilean Towns

13 Woe to you, Chorazin! Woe to you, Bethsaida! For if the wonders performed in you had taken place in Tyre and Sidon, they would have repented long ago, in sackcloth and ashes. *14* Yet for Tyre and Sidon it shall be more bearable at the judgment than for you. *15* And you, Capernaum, up to heaven will you be exalted? Into Hades shall you come down!

Q 10:13-15

Whoever Takes You in Takes Me in

16 Whoever takes you in takes me in, and whoever takes me in takes in the one who sent me.

Q 10:16

Thanksgiving that God Reveals Only to Children

21 At (that time) he said: I praise you, Father, Lord of heaven and earth, for you hid these things from sages and the learned, and disclosed them to children. Yes, Father, for that is what it has pleased you to do.

Q 10:21

Knowing the Father through the Son

22 Everything has been entrusted to me by my Father, and no one knows the Son except the Father, nor does anyone know the Father except the Son, and to whomever the Son chooses to reveal him.

Q 10:22

The Beatitude for the Eyes that See

23 Blessed are the eyes that see what you see .. . *24* For I tell you: Many prophets and kings wanted to see what you see, but never saw it, and to hear what you hear, but never heard it.

Q 10:23-24

The Lord's Prayer

2b When you pray, say: Father – may your name be kept holy! – let your reign come: *3* Our day's bread give us today; *4* and cancel our debts for us, as we too have cancelled for those in debt to us; and do not put us to the test!

Q 11:2b-4

The Certainty of the Answer to Prayer

9 I tell you: Ask and it will be given to you, search and you will find, knock and it will be opened to you. *10* For everyone who asks receives, and the one who searches finds, and to the one who knocks will it be opened. *11* .. What person of you, whose child asks for bread, will give him a stone? *12* Or again when he asks for a fish, will give him a snake? *13* So if you, though evil, know how to give good gifts to your children, by how much more will the Father from heaven give good things to those who ask him!

Q 11:9-13

Refuting the Beelzebul Accusation

14 And he cast out a demon which made a person mute. And once the demon was cast out, the mute person spoke. And the crowds were amazed. *15*But some said: By Beelzebul, the ruler of demons, he casts out demons! *17* But, knowing their thoughts, he said to them: Every kingdom divided against itself is left barren, and every household divided against itself will not stand. *18* And if Satan is divided against himself, how will his kingdom stand? *19* And if I by Beelzebul cast out demons, your sons, by whom do they cast them out? This is why they will be your judges. *20*But if it is by the finger of God that I cast out demons, then there has come upon you God's reign.

Q 11:14-15, 17-20

Looting a Strong Person

21 (A strong person's house cannot be looted, *22* but if someone still stronger overpowers him, he does get looted.)

Q 11:21-22

The One not with Me

23 The one not with me is against me, and the one not gathering with me scatters.

Q 11:23

The Return of the Unclean Spirit

24 When the defiling spirit has left the person, it wanders through waterless regions looking for a resting-place, and finds none. Then it says: I will return to my house from which I came. *25* And on arrival it finds it swept and tidied up. *26* Then it goes and brings with it seven other spirits more evil than itself, and, moving in, they settle there. And the last circumstances of that person become worse than the first.

Q 11:24-26

Hearing and Keeping God's Word
27-28 . .

Q 11:27-28

The Sign of Jonah for This Generation

16 But some .. were demanding from him a sign. *29* But .. he said ..: This generation is an evil .. generation; it demands a sign, but a sign will not be given to it − except the sign of Jonah! *30* For as Jonah became to the Ninevites a sign, so also will the son of humanity be to this generation.

Q 11:16, 29-30

Something More than Solomon and Jonah

31 The queen of the South will be raised at the judgment with this generation and condemn it, for she came from the ends of the earth to listen to the wisdom of Solomon, and look, something more than Solomon is here! *32*Ninevite men will arise at the judgment with this generation and condemn it. For they repented at the announcement of Jonah, and look, something more than Jonah is here!

Q 11:31-32

The Light on the Lampstand

33 No one lights a lamp and puts it in a hidden place, but on the lampstand, and it gives light for everyone in the house.

Q 11:33

The Jaundiced Eye Darkens the Body's Radiance

34 The lamp of the body is the eye. If your eye is generous, your whole body is radiant; but if your eye is jaundiced, your whole body is dark. *35*So if the light within you is dark, how great must the darkness be!

Q 11:34-35

Woes against the Pharisees

39a .. [42] Woe to you, Pharisees, for you tithe mint and dill and cumin, and give up justice and mercy and faithfulness. But these one had to do, without giving up those. [39b] Woe to you, Pharisees, for you purify the outside of the cup and dish, but inside they are full of plunder and dissipation. [41] Purify .. the inside of the cup, ... its outside ... pure. [43] Woe to you, Pharisees, for you love the place of honor at banquets and the front seat in the synagogues and accolades in the markets. [44] Woe to you, Pharisees, for you are like indistinct tombs and people walking on top are unaware.

Q 11:39a, 42, 39b, 41, 43-44

Woes against the Exegetes of the Law

46b And woe to you, exegetes of the Law, for you bind ... burdens, and load on the backs of people, but you yourselves do not want to lift your finger to move them. [52] Woe to you, exegetes of the Law, for you shut the kingdom of (God) from people; you did not go in, nor let in those trying to get in. [47] Woe to you, for you built the tombs of the prophets, but your forefathers killed them. [48] Thus you witness against yourselves that you are the sons of your forefathers.

..

Q 11:46b, 52, 47-48

Wisdom's Judgment on This Generation

49 Therefore also .. Wisdom said: I will send them prophets and sages, and some of them they will kill and persecute, *50* so that a settling of accounts for the blood of all the prophets poured out from the founding of the world may be required of this generation, *51* from the blood of Abel to the blood of Zechariah, murdered between the sacrificial altar and the House. Yes, I tell you: An accounting will be required of this generation!

Q 11:49-51

Proclaiming What Was Whispered

2 Nothing is covered up that will not be exposed, and hidden that will not be known. *3* What I say to you in the dark, speak in the light; and what you hear whispered in the ear, proclaim on the housetops.

Q 12:2-3

Not Fearing the Body's Death

4 And do not be afraid of those who kill the body, but cannot kill the soul. *5* But fear .. the one who is able to destroy both the soul and body in Gehenna.

Q 12:4-5

More Precious than Many Sparrows

6 Are not five sparrows sold for two cents? And yet not one of them will fall to earth without your Father's consent. *7* But even the hairs of your head all are numbered. Do not be afraid, you are worth more than many sparrows.

Q 12:6-7

Confessing or Denying

8 Anyone who may speak out for me in public, the son of humanity will also speak out for him before the angels ... . *9* But whoever may deny me in public will be denied before the angels .. .

Q 12:8-9

Speaking against the holy Spirit

10 And whoever says a word against the son of humanity, it will be forgiven him; but whoever speaks against the holy Spirit, it will not be forgiven him.

Q 12:10

Hearings before Synagogues

11 When they bring you before synagogues, do not be anxious about how or what you are to say; *12* for the holy Spirit will teach you in that .. hour what you are to say.

Q 12:11-12

Storing up Treasures in Heaven

33 Do not treasure for yourselves treasures on earth, where moth and gnawing deface and where robbers dig through and rob, but treasure for yourselves treasures in heaven, where neither moth nor gnawing defaces and where robbers do not dig through nor rob. *34* For where your treasure is, there will also be your heart.

Q 12:33-34

Free from Anxiety like Ravens and Lilies

22b Therefore I tell you, do not be anxious about your life, what you are to eat, nor about your body, with what you are to clothe yourself. *23* Is not life more than food, and the body than clothing? *24* Consider the ravens: They neither sow nor reap nor gather into barns, and yet God feeds them. Are you not better than the birds? *25* And who of you by being anxious is able to add to one's stature a .. cubit? *26* And why are you anxious about clothing? *27* Observe the lilies, how they grow: They do not work nor do they spin. Yet I tell you: Not even Solomon in all his glory was arrayed like one of these. *28* But if in the field the grass, there today and tomorrow thrown into the oven, God clothes thus, will he not much more clothe you, persons of petty faith! *29* So do not be anxious, saying: What are we to eat? Or: What are we to drink? Or: What are we to wear? *30* For all these the Gentiles seek; for your Father knows that you need them all. *31* But seek his kingdom, and all these shall be granted to you.   *Q 12:22b-31*

The Son of Humanity Comes as a Robber

39 But know this: If the householder had known in which watch the robber was coming, he would not have let his house be dug into. *40* You also must be ready, for the Son of Humanity is coming at an hour you do not expect.

Q 12:39-40

The Faithful or Unfaithful Slave

42 Who then is the faithful and wise slave whom the master put over his household to give them food on time? *43* Blessed is that slave whose master, on coming, will find so doing. *44* Amen, I tell you, he will appoint him over all his possessions. *45* But if that slave says in his heart: My master is delayed, and begins to beat his fellow slaves, and eats and drinks with the drunkards, *46* the master of that slave will come on a day he does not expect and at an hour he does not know, and will cut him to pieces and give him an inheritance with the faithless.

Q 12:42-46

Children against Parents

49 Fire have I come to hurl on the earth, and how I wish it had already blazed up! *51* Do you think that I have come to hurl peace on earth? I did not come to hurl peace, but a sword! *53* For I have come to divide son against father, and daughter against her mother, and daughter-in-law against her mother-in-law.

Q 12:49, 51, 53

Judging the Time

54 But he said to them: When evening has come, you say: Good weather! For the sky is flame red. [55] And at dawn: Today it's wintry! For the lowering sky is flame red. [56] The face of the sky you know to interpret, but the time you are not able to?

Q 12:54-56

Settling out of Court

58 While you go along with your opponent on the way, make an effort to get loose from him, lest the opponent hand you over to the judge, and the judge to the assistant, and the (assistant) throw you into prison. [59] I say to you: You will not get out of there until you pay the last penny!

Q 12:58-59

The Mustard Seed

18 What is the kingdom of God like, and with what am I to compare it? [19] It is like a seed of mustard, which a person took and threw into his garden. And it grew and developed into a tree, and the birds of the sky nested in its branches.

Q 13:18-19

The Yeast

20 And again: With what am I to compare the kingdom of God? *21* It is like yeast, which a woman took and hid in three measures of flour until it was fully fermented.

Q 13:20-21

I Do not Know You

24 Enter through the narrow door, for many will seek to enter and few are those who (enter through) it. *25* When the householder has arisen and locked the door, and you begin to stand outside and knock on the door, saying: Master, open for us, and he will answer you: I do not know you, *26* then you will begin saying: We ate in your presence and drank, and it was in our streets you taught. *27* And he will say to you: I do not know you! Get away from me, you who do lawlessness!

Q 13:24-27

Many Shall Come from Sunrise and Sunset

29 And many shall come from Sunrise and Sunset and recline *28* with Abraham and Isaac and Jacob in the kingdom of God, but you will be thrown out into the outer darkness, where there will be wailing and grinding of teeth.

Q 13:29, 28

The Reversal of the Last and the First

30 .. The last will be first, and the first last.

Q 13:30

Judgment over Jerusalem

34 O Jerusalem, Jerusalem, who kills the prophets and stones those sent to her! How often I wanted to gather your children together, as a hen gathers her nestlings under her wings, and you were not willing! *35* Look, your house is forsaken! .. I tell you: You will not see me until (the time) comes when you say: Blessed is the one who comes in the name of the Lord!

Q 13:34-35

The Exalted Humbled and the Humble Exalted

11 Everyone exalting oneself will be humbled, and the one humbling oneself will be exalted.

Q 14:11

The Invited Dinner Guests

16 A certain person prepared a large dinner, and invited many. *17* And he sent his slave at the time of the dinner to say to the invited: Come, for it is now ready. *18* (One declined because of his) farm. *19* (Another declined because of his business.) *20* .. *21* (And the slave, on coming, said) these things to his master. Then the householder, enraged, said to his slave: *23* Go out on the roads, and whomever you find, invite, so that my house may be filled.

Q 14:16-18, 19-20?, 21, 23

Hating One's Family

26 (The one who) does not hate father and mother (can)not (be) my (disciple); and (the one who does not hate) son and daughter cannot be my disciple.

Q 14:26

Taking One's Cross

27 .. The one who does not take one's cross and follow after me cannot be my disciple.

Q 14:27

Finding or Losing One's Life

33 The one who finds one's life will lose it, and the one who loses one's life for my sake will find it.

Q 17:33

Insipid Salt

34 Salt is good; but if salt becomes insipid, with what will it be seasoned? *35* Neither for the earth nor for the dunghill is it fit — it gets thrown out.

Q 14:34-35

God or Mammon

13 Nobody can serve two masters; for a person will either hate the one and love the other, or be devoted to the one and despise the other. You cannot serve God and Mammon.

Q 16:13

Since John the Kingdom of God

16 .. The law and the prophets were until John. From then on the kingdom of God is violated and the violent plunder it.

Q 16:16

No Serif of the Law to Fall

17 But it is easier for heaven and earth to pass away than for one iota or one serif of the law to fall.

Q 16:17

Divorce Leading to Adultery

18 Everyone who divorces his wife and marries another commits adultery, and the one who marries a divorcée commits adultery.

Q 16:18

Against Enticing Little Ones

1 It is necessary for enticements to come, but woe to the one through whom they come! *2* It is better for him if a millstone is put around his neck and he is thrown into the sea, than that he should entice one of these little ones.

Q 17:1-2

The Lost Sheep

4 Which person is there among you who has a hundred sheep, on losing one of them, will not leave the ninety-nine in the mountains and go hunt for the lost one? *5a* And if it should happen that he finds it, *7* I say to you that he rejoices over it more than over the ninety-nine that did not go astray.

Q 15:4-5a, 7

The Lost Coin

8 Or what woman who has ten coins, if she were to lose one coin, would not light a lamp and sweep the house and hunt until she finds? *9* And on finding she calls the friends and neighbors, saying: Rejoice with me, for I found the coin which I had lost. *10* Just so, I tell you, there is joy before the angels over one repenting sinner.

Q 15:8-10

Forgiving a Sinning Brother Repeatedly

3 If your brother sins against you, rebuke him; and if he repents, forgive him. *4* And if seven times a day he sins against you, also seven times shall you forgive him.

Q 17:3-4

Faith like a Mustard Seed

6 If you have faith like a mustard seed, you might say to this mulberry tree: Be uprooted and planted in the sea! And it would obey you.

Q 17:6

The Kingdom of God within You

20 But on being asked when the kingdom of God is coming, he answered them and said: The kingdom of God is not coming visibly. *21* Nor will one say: Look, here! or: There! For, look, the kingdom of God is within you!

Q 17:20-21

The Son of Humanity like Lightning

23 If they say to you: Look, he is in the wilderness, do not go out; look, he is indoors, do not follow. *24* For as the lightning streaks out from Sunrise and flashes as far as Sunset, so will the Son of Humanity be on his day.

Q 17:23-24

Vultures around a Corpse

37 Wherever the corpse, there the vultures will gather.   *Q 17:37*

As in the Days of Noah

26 .. As it took place in the days of Noah, so will it be in the day of the Son of Humanity. *27* For as in those days they were eating and drinking, marrying and giving in marriage, until the day Noah entered the ark and the flood came and took them all, *28-29* .. *30*so will it also be on the day the Son of Humanity is revealed.

Q 17:26-27, 28-29, 30

One Taken, One Left

34 I tell you: There will be two men in the field; one is taken and one is left. *35*Two women will be grinding at the mill; one is taken and one is left.

Q 17:34-35

The Entrusted Money

12 .. A certain person, on taking a trip, *13* called ten of his slaves and gave them ten minas and said to them: Do business until I come. *15* .. After a long time the master of those slaves comes and settles accounts with them. *16* And the first came saying: Master, your mina has produced ten more minas. *17* And he said to him: Well done, good slave, you have been faithful over a little, I will set you over much. ¹⁸ And the second came saying: Master, your mina has earned five minas. ¹⁹ He said to him: Well done, good slave, you have been faithful over a little, I will set you over much. ²⁰ And the other came saying: Master, ²¹ I knew you, that you are a hard person, reaping where you did not sow and gathering up from where you did not winnow; and, scared, I went and hid your (mina) in the ground. Here, you have what belongs to you. ²² He said to him: Wicked slave! You knew that I reap where I have not sown, and gather up from where I have not winnowed? ²³ Then you had to invest my money with the money changers! And at my coming I would have received what belongs to me plus interest. ²⁴ So take from him the mina and give it to the one who has the ten minas. ²⁶ For to everyone who has will be given; but from the one who does not have, even what he has will be taken from him.

Q 19:12-13, 15-24, 26

You Will Judge the Twelve Tribes of Israel

28 .. You who have followed me ³⁰ will sit .. on thrones judging the twelve tribes of Israel.

Q 22:28, 30

*   *   *   *   *

Further Reading

There is an extensive bibliography in other languages, especially German, which is omitted here, and only a small selection of English literature is included. For a complete bibliography one may consult F. Neirynck, J. Verheyden, and R. Corstjens, *The Gospel of Matthew and the Gospel Source Q: A Cumulative Bibliography 1950–1995* (2 vols., BETL 140; Leuven: Leuven University Press and Peeters, 1998); or David M. Scholer, *Q Bibliography, Twentieth Century* (Documenta Q: Supplementum; Leuven: Peeters, 2001).

For the text of Q in Greek and English, and in the context of a synopsis of the Gospels, see James M. Robinson, Paul Hoffmann, and John S. Kloppenborg, general editors, Milton C. Moreland, managing editor, *The Critical Edition of Q: Synopsis, including the Gospels of Matthew and Luke, Mark and Thomas, with English, German, and French Translations of Q and Thomas* (Minneapolis: Fortress Press; and Leuven: Peeters, 2000), and in shortened form in *The Sayings Gospel Q in Greek and English with Parallels from the Gospels of Mark and Thomas.* Leuven: Peeters, 2001; and Minneapolis: Fortress Press, 2002.

*   *   *   *   *

Kloppenborg, John S. 1987. *The Formation of Q: Trajectories in Ancient Wisdom Collections.* Studies in Antiquity and Christianity. Philadelphia: Fortress Press. (Reprint: Harrisburg, Penn.: Trinity Press International, 2000.)

————. 1988. *Q Parallels: Synopsis, Critical Notes, and Concordance.* Foundations and Facets: New Testament. Sonoma, Calif.: Polebridge.

————, ed. 1994. *The Shape of Q: Signal Essays on the Sayings Gospel.* Minneapolis: Fortress Press.

————, ed. 1995. *Conflict and Invention: Literary, Rhetorical, and Social Studies on the Sayings Gospel Q.* Valley Forge, Penn.: Trinity Press International.

*Kloppenborg Verbin, John S. 2000. *Excavating Q: The History and Setting of the Sayings Gospel.* Minneapolis: Fortress Press; and Edinburgh: T & T Clark.

Lindemann, Andreas, ed. 2001. *The Sayings Source Q and the Historical Jesus*. Bibliotheca ephemeridum theologicarum lovaniensium 158. Leuven: Leuven University Press and Peeters.

Piper, Ronald A., ed. 1995. *The Gospel behind the Gospels: Current Studies on Q*. Supplements to Novum Testamentum 75. Leiden: Brill.

Robinson, James M. and Helmut Koester. 1971, paperback 1979. *Trajectories through Early Christianity*. Philadelphia: Fortress Press.

Theissen, Gerd. 1992, 1993. *Social Reality and the Early Christians: Theology, Ethics, and the World of the New Testament*. Translated by Margaret Kohl. Minneapolis: Fortress Press; and Edinburgh: T. & T. Clark.

Tuckett, Christopher M. 1996. *Q and the History of Early Christianity: Studies on Q*. Edinburgh: T. & T. Clark; and Peabody, Mass.: Hendrickson.

Uro, Risto, ed. 1996. *Symbols and Strata: Essays on the Sayings Gospel Q*. Suomen Eksegeettisen Seuran Julkaisuja. Publications of the Finnish Exegetical Society 65; Helsinki: Finnish Exegetical Society; and Göttingen: Vandenhoeck & Ruprecht.

FACETS